YOUR GUIDE TO

NOT GETTING MURDERED

IN A QUAINT

ENGLISH VILLAGE

LONDON
OXF

YOUR GUIDE TO

Not Getting Murdered in a Quaint English Village

MAUREEN JOHNSON
& JAY COOPER

TEN SPEED PRESS
California | New York

Published in the United States by Ten Speed Press, an imprint of Random House, a division of Penguin Random House LLC, New York.
www.tenspeed.com

Library of Congress Cataloging-in-Publication Data
Names: Johnson, Maureen, 1973- author. | Cooper, Jay, 1974- illustrator.
Title: Your guide to not getting murdered in a quaint English village / Maureen Johnson and Jay Cooper.
Description: First edition. | California : Ten Speed Press, [2021]
Identifiers: LCCN 2020054601 (print) | LCCN 2020054602 (ebook) | ISBN 9781984859624 (hardcover) | ISBN 9781984859631 (ebook)
Subjects: LCSH: Villages--England--Humor. | Murder--Humor. | Television programs--Humor.
Classification: LCC PN6231.V536 J64 2021 (print) | LCC PN6231.V536 (ebook) | DDC 818/.602--dc23
LC record available at https://lccn.loc.gov/2020054601
LC ebook record available at https://lccn.loc.gov/2020054602

Hardcover ISBN: 978-1-9848-5962-4
eBook ISBN: 978-1-9848-5963-1

Printed in China

Acquiring Editor: Paul Whitlatch | Project Editor: Katie Berry |
Production Editor: Shaida Boroumand
Designer/Art Director: Lizzie Allen
Production Manager: Dan Myers
Copyeditor: Jeff Campbell | Proofreader: Mikayla Butchart
Publicist: Leilani Zee | Marketer: Daniel Wikey

10 9 8

First Edition

CONTENTS

It is my belief, Watson, founded upon my experience, that the lowest and vilest alleys in London do not present a more dreadful record of sin than does the smiling and beautiful countryside.

–SHERLOCK HOLMES,

"The Adventure of the Copper Beeches"
by Arthur Conan Doyle

A Note to the Gentle Reader

It's happened. You've finally taken that dream trip to England. You have seen Big Ben, Buckingham Palace, and Hyde Park. You have ridden in one of London's famous black cabs and encountered the Beefeaters at the Tower of London and the ravens under their care. You have taken the Jack the Ripper tour and walked those bloody footsteps in East London. This should be enough for anyone–but, perhaps, not enough for you. You've decided to leave the hustle and bustle of the city to stretch your legs in the bucolic countryside of these green and pleasant lands.

You've read the books and watched the shows. You know what to expect: You'll drink a pint in the sunny courtyard of a local pub. You'll wander down charming alleyways between stone cottages. Residents will tip their flatcaps at you as they bicycle along cobblestone streets. It will be idyllic.

The author respectfully suggests you put aside these fantasies. It is possible that you will find yourself in a placid and tedious little corner of England; it is just as possible that you will end up in an English Murder Village. You will not know you are in a Murder Village, as they look like all other villages. When you arrive in Shrimpling or Pickles-in-the-Woods or Wombat-on-Sea or wherever it is, there will be no immediate signs of danger. This is exactly the problem. You are already in the trap.

My advice: Stick to urban areas. Do not go to the countryside. Dispose of this book, and continue on with your life.

If you still insist on pursuing this course of action, commit the following information to memory. It may help you remain alive, if anything can.

Regretfully yours,

The Author

The VILLAGE
To Manor
Pond
Inn
The Old Mill
Farm

illage Hall
Church
Churchyard
Police Station
Courthouse
Village Shop
Antique Shop
Pub

THE VILLAGE

The village is comprised of two major parts: the village proper and the manor just outside of it. At one time, the residents of the manor likely owned the village ground and exerted control over the villagers and all that they produced. Fortunately, we have rid ourselves of such barbaric economic structures.

In olden times, you would have arrived in a rumbling carriage, or perhaps by foot, tired and sore from the journey. Perhaps today you will arrive by train, that most murdery of conveyances. Or you may come by car, wincing as it makes its way along the far too narrow country roads, the hedgerows brushing the doors as you pass. The city is behind you now. The village is ahead.

All villages are an idyll of stone cottages, cheery whitewashed storefronts, winding streets, and artfully overgrown gardens. Of course, in a Murder Village, those whitewashed buildings and stone structures are a mouthful of smiling teeth that consume the unwise and the unlucky, whose chewed remains are pressed through those streets that wind and twist through the town like a gastrointestinal tract. The gardens absorb what remains.

Forewarned is forearmed.

Buildings & Spaces

English villages follow an ancient blueprint from a simpler time, when babies drank beer and everyone had a sheep. Time may march on elsewhere, but not in the village. They don't like change in the village.

THE VILLAGE CHURCH

A village has to have a church; those are the rules. For hundreds of years, the village church has been the center of village life and death, with emphasis on the last one. It is the biggest, grandest, highest building around. It has fonts to drown in, vaults to be sealed in, a bell tower to fall from, and an altar to be sacrificed on. The vicar will find your body if you venture here.

THE CHURCHYARD

Behind the village church. Literally the village body dump. It's full of headstones of various ages, some crooked and sinking into the earth, and some still covered in fresh stonecutting dust. Someone's always going in at night to leave flowers or keys or letters—or any combination of the three. It's busier than the train station. Technically you're supposed to be dead before you end up here, but villagers aren't strict about this.

THE PUB

Everyone loves the pub. Locals gather here at any time of day to enjoy a pint of the famous local cider and have a chat. You, however, are not a local. The moment you enter the pub, you will be observed from every corner. Your habits, demeanor, and manner of dress will be studied. You are an insect that has flown into the spider's web. You will be wound in a fabric of pleasant conversation as you are consumed. The cider is very good, though, with a mineral-rich aftertaste. How do they get flavor like that?

THE VILLAGE SHOP

It sells cheese, stamps, tea, and death.

THE VILLAGE POND

Those ducks didn't get fat on bread.

THE VILLAGE HALL

All villages have a hall—an all-purpose building where every kind of festivity, meeting, or event is held. Every villager goes into the hall at some point or other. Their fingerprints are up and down the walls. The floral society goes toe to toe with the amateur dramatic society. The watercolor painting class encounters the jujitsu class on the stairs. Harsh words are spoken about other villagers' poetry, their undrinkable home brew, and their Morris dancing skills. The village hall is a factory where petty grudges are made, and there is no grudge like a petty, hobby-related grudge. Oh, you giggled at Edith's sonnet? Sounds like someone's about to be found clubbed to death with a typewriter, their mouth stuffed full of poems.

THE VILLAGE INN

The inn's business model is set up to accommodate all of the mysterious figures with pulled-down hats and scarves over their faces who pay in cash and won't come out of their rooms, even for meals. On the average night, the rooms are occupied by visiting inspectors from Scotland Yard, blackmailers, people long thought dead, and people who are actually dead.

THE VILLAGE GREEN

Why is it so *spongy*?

THE FANCY ANTIQUE SHOP

The antique shop is always closed. The owner is always away. The wares displayed in the window are priceless and covered with dust. This is not a sustainable business model, and yet the business remains afloat. Everyone knows how but no one talks about it. Don't ask them about it. *Stop asking questions.*

THE POLICE STATION

It's just a mug of tea in a cupboard. There is only one constable, which is unfortunate, what with all the murders and everything.

ANYWHERE WITH A VAT

In English Murder Villages, vats exist for the express purpose of drowning people—in beer, in pickling brine, in whiskey, in jam. This is doubly true if the vat was built by fourteenth-century monks. If anyone offers to show you their vat, say you need to get something from your car, start the engine, and run them over. The constable understands this sort of thing. Tell him about the vat.

THE OLD MILL

It's not where murders happen, but for some reason it's often why.

The Residents of the Village

A village is not its buildings or its land; sadly, a village is the sum of its people. Eliminate the people and the problem is gone. Except that the problem is largely the elimination of people.

THE TOWN DOCTOR

The doctor is up in everyone's business and must die, along with anyone foolish enough to pay them a visit. You don't need a doctor. You have the internet.

THE NEWEST RESIDENT

They don't know the Old Ways and refuse to learn. They want to open up a yoga and sound healing studio in that twee Grade Two-listed thatched cottage. They're talking to you because no one else will talk to them. They'll be dead soon enough.

THE OLDEST RESIDENT

They're the hardest to kill for a reason.

THE PUBLICAN

"We brew our own. Would you care to see our vat?"

THE VILLAGE GOSSIP

"You won't *believe* what I just saw! Fiona was at the pub and . . . just a moment. There's someone at the door. I'll set the phone down and be right back. Coming!"

THE AMATEUR ASTRONOMER

They like to wander alone to remote locations at night with a big looking-tube to look. Draw a circle around every word in that sentence that means "no."

THE BIRD-WATCHER

Birds are related to dinosaurs. Did you know that? And like the dinosaur, the birdwatcher will soon be extinct because *looking*.

ANYONE WHO LOOKS OUT WINDOWS

It's curtains for you.

THE TRAINSPOTTER

"Why, yes, this carriage is from the 1984 stock and has thirty seats. It used to come in from London, Waterloo Station, but when they redid the tracks in 1998, why I'll show you right here is where they connected the two, this rail right here . . . oh no, there goes my head."

THE THESPIAN

They quote Shakespeare in public. To children.

THE VILLAGE CONSTABLE

"We haven't had a murder in this village since . . . oh dear, there's been another one."

THE VISITING MYSTERY NOVELIST

You'll make nice story meat.

ANYONE WHO LEAVES A MESSAGE

All messages in a Murder Village are bad news. It means someone Knows Something. Don't leave messages. Don't hang around people who do.

THE GARDENER

The roses are perfect because of all the people under them.

THE FARMER

Constantly fielding offers from city folk who want to turn the farmland into a shopping center and *fielding* those same city folk who want to turn the farmland into a shopping center.

THE PERSON WHO OPENS THE DOOR AND SAYS, "OH, IT'S YOU"

Well, they were right.

THE VICAR

See also: the Village Church. When you see the vicar, run. If you are not dead yet, the vicar is obliged to kill you.

Village Events

Villages are built on traditions. Since the times of old, they have observed the rites. Some of the details have changed, but the song remains much the same. Birth, death, planting, death, harvest, death, springtime, death, sports, death . . .

THE VILLAGE FÊTE

The village fête is a fair, a celebration on the village green. Residents toss coconuts, judge cakes, drink tea, and whack toy rats with mallets. It's a nice way to spend a summer's day and thin out the local population, because where there is a fête, there is murder. If you enter a town while the fête is happening, you are already dead. The teapots are brimming with poison. The sponge cakes are full of glass. There's an axe in the fortune-telling tent. The coconuts are bombs. It's like the Hunger Games, but dangerous.

£
5,000

CRICKET

What a lovely English pastime! A sport where the players wear nice white sweaters, the matches go on for five days, and everyone drinks large quantities of tea and gin. The terminology is so quaint! Wickets, pudding, bunny, teapot, lollipop . . . Just a lovely, civilized time, with players running around a squishy green field with paddle-shaped bats, whacking a rock-hard ball, thinking about how much they resent their teammates. The highest trophy in the cricketing world is literally an urn full of ashes, so you can't pretend you weren't warned.

HARVEST SEASON

The villagers are proud of their local cider, and rightly so. It's the soil around these parts, you see, and the apple trees of the orchard must be refreshed from time to time with the blood of . . . you'll do.

THE HISTORICAL REENACTMENT

Villagers love to remember the glorious old days, when they used to skewer one another with sticks, fire muskets into one another's faces, and cut off their neighbors' heads in the name of king or country or whatever they were into back then. To commemorate these wonderful times, villagers will occasionally put on moth-eaten clothes and big hats and run around a field with dull pikes and unloaded weapons to show everyone how very grand it was to bleed out in the mud just

behind the pub. It should go without saying that one of the pikes will be sharpened, and some of the guns will be loaded. If you absolutely insist on attending the reenactment, do not attend the reenactment. Do not let your vigilance end there, though. The reenactment is often a misdirect. Another victim will die doing something normal in another part of the village while everyone else is playing murder in a field. So don't not go to the reenactment, either.

FUNERALS

There are a lot of these. They may seem safe because the death has already happened, but there is often a "since we've already dug a hole" spirit about these events. Locals have learned to economize.

VILLAGE QUIZ

Let's see how well you have absorbed the material so far. One of the following scenarios is safe. Can you spot which one?

1. You have arrived a week before the village fête. Everyone is preparing their jams, cakes, scones, buns, and chutneys. This is a trial run before the big event, and the perennial winning baker wants an impartial person to sample their wares. You, stranger, will you be so kind as to taste this elderberry and lemon cake? Just a small piece to see if it is too sweet?

---

2. You've arrived just in time for the "Village of the Year" competition! A television network has come to make Normal-on-Toast and Frampling battle it out and prove once and for all which village has the best tea shop or the shiniest fish or the most Morris dancers. All the villagers are putting the finishing touches on their gardens, setting out the good china, and placing their ducks in the pond. Would you like to appear on camera saying how wonderful the village is?

3. What could be more wonderful than listening to the bells of the village church ringing out over a clear summer morning? The vicar wants to know if you would like to climb up the bell tower to see how they are rung. You'll get the best view from up there. You can see the manor. Why, you can see half the county! Come up, won't you, to ring a bell?

You must choose one or the vicar will kill you by default.

The answer is number three. You must go to the bell tower with the vicar.

In the case of number one, the person offering you the cake has nothing against you personally. They've poisoned their rival's test cake in the hopes of killing a stranger. You can't bake the winning cake if you're in jail for murder. The cake is death. Do not eat the cake. ☠

Number two sounds safe, but do not be fooled. The Village of the Year is an open call to war. The moment you open your mouth to say how much you enjoyed your scone in Frampling, a grandmotherly woman from Normal-on-Toast will pass by and insert a knitting needle directly through your neck. She cannot be arrested for this. All is legal in the Village of the Year competition. Technically, this counts as a craft. ☠

You must go to the bell tower. You have no choice. You must kill the vicar. Sometimes, the murderer is you.

The MANOR
Pond
Hedge Maze
The Folly
Gatehouse
N
E
S
W

Statuary
Apiary
Chapel
e West Wing
Greenhouse
The East Wing
Kennel
The Stables

THE MANOR

At one time, wealth came from the land, and those who owned the land were all-powerful. The manor sat apart from the village that was the source of its wealth. Back then, there was a servant for every whim, ensuring that the manor-dwellers never had to answer their own doors, run their own baths, brush their own hair, or find their own ducks to kill.

The manor is not a house or a home; it is an extension of a biological line, a symbol of dynastic power. Now it stands–barely–a shell of its former glory. The manor is too expensive to maintain in the modern world, now that people are so fussy about "working conditions" and "salary." The poor aristocrat is a geode of privilege and anger–what you end up with if you compress all of the entitlement and rage of a collapsed empire into solid matter. They've had to sell the lesser Turners and the staff is down to eight. Most of the income is derived from tourists who have come to watch the manor crumble to dust.

Buildings & Spaces

The manor is not a single house; it is a collection of buildings, structures, and outdoor areas. All parts of the manor function as one strange organism–a biome, if you will, designed to support the lifestyles of the idle rich.

THE HOUNDS

If you arrive after dark, assume the dogs will eat you. Don't believe the old chestnut that you can just toss them a steak and win them over. These dogs have been eating leftover servants for years and have developed a taste for tender human flesh. Here's what they haven't experienced: real love. Throw them a tennis ball. Ask them, who's a good girl? When you leave, if you leave, take the dogs with you. They deserve better.

THE GATEHOUSE

"They used to let orphans stay here, you know. To work in the kitchen and clean the chimneys. They lived in the cottage back in Victorian times. There were little children all over the place then. Not sure what happened to them. I believe there was an inquiry . . ."

THE STABLES

How would you prefer to go: pitchforked or trampled by a two-thousand-pound animal? Spoiler: It will be both.

STATUARY

They look so real, don't they? So very real.
Almost as if they're made of actual people.

STIFF & GREY'S QUIK-DRY CEMENT
VENUS

THE GREENHOUSE

You'd think a building made entirely of glass would be easy to see into, but it's impossible to get a look inside. The vines grow all the way to the ceiling and seem to be moving in rhythm. Are they... dancing?

THE FOLLY

It's a small, fake temple at the far side of the pond, perfect for picnics, trysts, and casual strangulations.

THE APIARY

"We produce our own honey here! Makes a profit for the manor, you know. Keeps us afloat. Best honey in the county! All organic! Come see the bees! The bees! *The precious bees.*"

THE POND

Full of the skeletons of Victorian children and, if you are unwise, you.

THE HEDGE MAZE

You don't find the way out—it finds you.

Rooms & Architecture

The interior of the main house is a puzzle box of danger, built and redesigned so many times over the years that no one knows what the real layout is. It is madness, secrecy, and familial hatred made manifest. Certain general precautions can be given.

HIGHER FLOORS

Stay low. They can't throw you off the balcony if you never go up there. Try the stairs.

THE STAIRS

They are the xylophones of death.

LOWER FLOORS

Marble busts and giant vases fall down, not up. Get to higher ground.

THE FLOORS IN GENERAL

They're fine if you know where the weak spots and holes are. On the bright side, you'll bypass the stairs.

THE ATTIC

Good idea. Save time. Go right to the ghost part of the house.

THE BASEMENT

No one can drop a bust or vase on you here, and there is nowhere lower to go. It must be safe. Wait. Who turned the lights out? Was this wall here a minute ago? Is this some kind of vault? Hello? Can anyone hear me?

THE KITCHEN

No.

THE PANTRY

"You must try the honey! It's produced by the manor's very own bees! The bees! *The precious bees!* What golden goodness they have given us! We must go and thank the *bees . . .*"

WILL
WILL

THE STUDY

It's for working on memoirs and revising wills.
You're mentioned in both, but not in a good way.

THE GUN ROOM

Strangely, it's safer than the study.

THE LIBRARY

It's best not to pull books down at random.
Things . . . happen sometimes.

CURSES

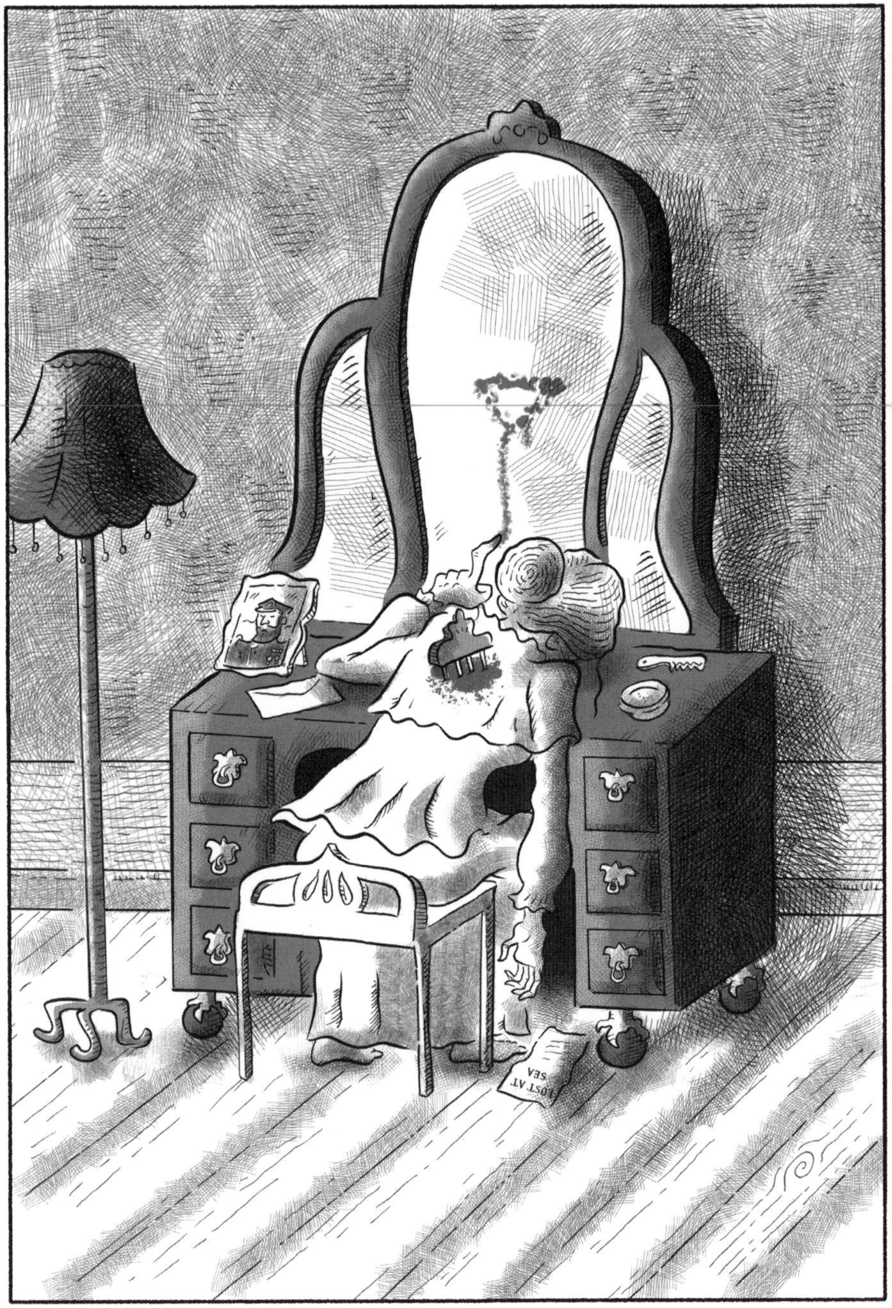
LOST AT
SEA

THE BEDROOMS

At the manor, you never sleep alone.

THE BATHROOM

Tired: the 100-year-old plumbing that feeds the bathtub.
Wired: the electricity to the 100-year-old plumbing that feeds the bathtub.

THE LOCKED ROOM

"Oh, that room? You wouldn't be interested in what's in there. It's very unique but not your sort of thing at all. But if you'd really like to see for yourself . . ."

Furnishings & Features

Obviously, each manor house has its own particular furnishings, but some elements are universal.

PAINTINGS

It's not just the eyes that move.

WALLS

All the best stuff happens inside of them.

CHIMNEYS

Orphan storage.

GRANDFATHER CLOCKS

Bong, bong, bong, *bang*. In you go.

A Red, Red Ribbon

THE PIANO

It's covered in photographs of relatives from many generations. So much family history! You can see the resemblances. Such strong resemblances. Really, really strong. Wait . . . is that Marianne at Queen Elizabeth's coronation? Is that James in a World War I uniform? Why are the twins in this photograph of a biplane? Who is in the pilot's seat? He looks just like the twins. And that's Reginald in this daguerrotype, surrounded by Victorian orphans, out by the cottage. How is that possible? Why is he the only one in the picture whose eyes haven't been scribbled out?

CANOPY BEDS

They have snakes in them.

THAT SUIT OF ARMOR, THE ONE WITHOUT A SWORD

Unlikely to kill you. It doesn't even have a sword. Wait. Didn't it have a sword before? Anyway, this is where they put your body after you've been murdered in order to surprise and terrify the others, so there's really no point in worrying about it. See also: That Suit of Armor, the One with the Sword.

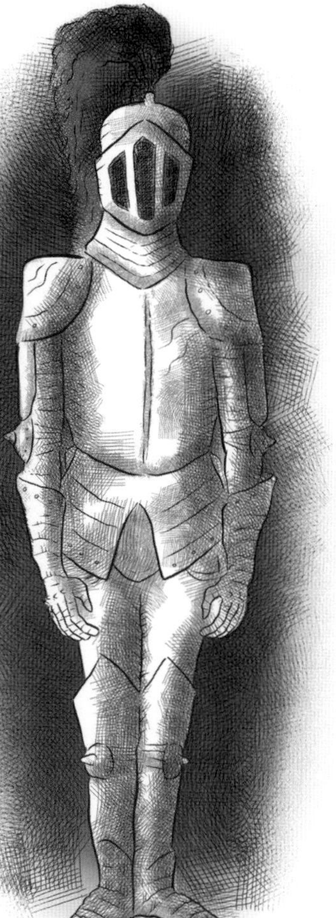

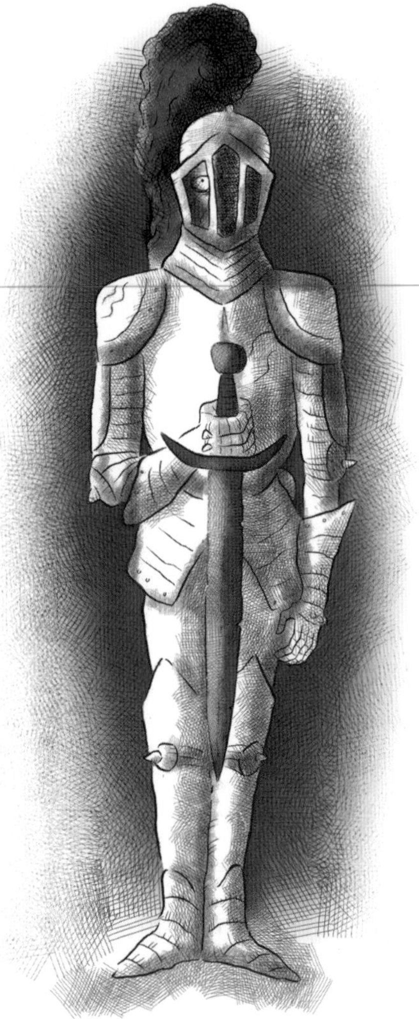

THAT SUIT OF ARMOR, THE ONE WITH THE SWORD

You're about to be stabbed and put in this suit of armor to surprise and terrify the others. The sword will then be removed, which will alarm everyone when they realize it is missing. See also: That Suit of Armor, the One without a Sword.

The Residents of the Manor

The manor has been handed down over the generations. The residents will often refer to their family tree, but "tree" is not quite the right word for this gnarled and stunted biological formation. They are too proud and too cash-strapped to live anywhere else or with anyone else, so they reside under one unstable roof, waiting to see which of them will be the last one standing.

THE PATRIARCH

He's delighted to see you! Come in, come in! He was just revising his will, cleaning his guns, feeding the puma, and drinking the contents of every half-empty cup in the building. Do you like deadly snakes? Come, come! You must fondle some before lunch. Mind you don't trip into this basket of knives. Who left that there? Anyway, follow him up the rickety ladder to the roof. Snakes love roofs.

THE MATRIARCH

She hates everyone, for good reason. Carries a loaded gun at all times. Has a parrot, Humphrey, who spies on the others. Leaves half-empty cups laced with poison all over the house, but damn it, this only seems to make him *stronger*. He's on the roof again, isn't he?

MARIANNE, THE OLDEST CHILD

Cries a lot. Didn't want to marry James, but what else could she *do*? *You* understand, don't you?

JAMES, MARIANNE'S HUSBAND

"Oh, I say, Marianne! There you are! The most ghastly thing has happened! I've swallowed a postage stamp! Is that illegal? I mean to say, *her* face—Her Majesty's face—is in my tum tum and that means it must come out the bum bum and that can't be legal, can it? To have *her* face be in *that* place?"

PENELOPE, THE MIDDLE CHILD

Speaks eighteen languages. Is a cardiac surgeon and a qualified pilot. Has seven lovers. Keeps a whip on her belt and a knife in her boot. Works in the greenhouse a lot, always at night. Feeds the parrot a string of lies. Is watching you.

ROGER, THE YOUNGEST CHILD, AND THE NEXT LORD OF THE MANOR

Dresses like Philip II of Spain. Lives in a tree in the garden. Has a pet toaster. Ate one of his own fingers to see if it was as crunchy as it looked. Is Minister of Agriculture.

UNCLE HENRY, THE PATRIARCH'S YOUNGER BROTHER, THE ONE WHO INHERITED NOTHING

He's still angry about what happened at the mill. Will have his revenge.

RUPERT AND PETER, THE TWINS

Always out of money. Spend all their time and resources on tennis, gambling, and cars. Materialize whenever cocktails are served or wills are mentioned. Everyone in the family seems to remember something about triplets, but Rupert and Peter insist there was never a third one.

AUNT CLARA

Lives on the top floor. Takes all of her meals in her room. No one is allowed inside, not even the maid. A servant once looked through the keyhole, then ran screaming from the building and was never seen again. Occasionally emerges just after dusk to stand in the doorway of the dining room and tell everyone how they are going to die.

COUSIN LUCY

Oh, she's *such* a sillybucket, isn't she? Don't mind her. She's no one. She's nothing. She'll get you another cup of tea. She should have offered earlier! She'll do it right now! Oh, she's tripped. Isn't that just like her! Step over her. Step *on* her. Wipe your feet on her. She wants you to. Oh, she's *such* a numpkins! She's mislaid her basket of knives again. Have you seen it? Stupid, *stupid* Lucy!

REGINALD, THE CHILD

Hangs out in the walls, keeps spiders in bottles, studies nineteenth-century dental procedures, collects lithographs of major historical fires.

HUMPHREY, A PARROT

Come to the greenhouse! Squalkkkk! There's candy in the greenhouse!
Squalkkkkk! Money under the floor of the greenhouse!
Squalkkkk! Don't be afraid of the greenhouse!

Frequent Guests

Certain people seem to turn up at the manor more than most. They all have their reasons, none of them good.

THE SPINSTER

"You know, when preparing mummies, the ancient Egyptians used to remove human brains with a gadget that looked just like this crochet hook. I think the old ways are best, don't you?"

THE COLONEL

Was in the war, you know. Isn't sure which war specifically.

THE PRIVATE DOCTOR

"Ah, I see you broke a nail. Looks like *someone* needs an injection of morphine."

THE NATURALIST

Was last seen running into the hedge maze with a net, chasing a *Lycaena virgaureae*. It's unclear who or what was chasing him. Isn't nature wonderful?

THE ARTIST

"I painted her at her most beautiful. Did you know, she died the next day? Terrible accident. Something to do with scissors. Dreadful. So many of my subjects have died so soon after I painted them. It's just lucky, I suppose, that I captured them on canvas right before they left us . . ."

THE ACTRESS

She's taking a break before her next big role, as she has been for the last eight years. Is desperate enough to marry Roger, if it comes to it. Or Humphrey.

THE FORMER GOVERNESS

Changed the nappies of every single person in this family, including Aunt Clara, so is entitled to come and stay as often as she likes, as much as she likes. This means all the time and for a long time. Drinks sherry at breakfast. Smokes cigars in her room. Has a deck of dirty playing cards for playing solitaire. No one knows how old she is. Keeps referring to "all those naughty orphans I had to send upstairs."

The Staff

Unlike regular people, the residents of the manor require others to help them perform basic tasks. One simply cannot do without servants. There used to be many more, but times are hard. The ones that remain are loyal or desperate or both.

MACKENZIE, THE PRIVATE SECRETARY

"I've served this family for two hundred and thirty . . .
I mean, twenty years."

FLORA, THE UPSTAIRS MAID

She knows what happened at the mill.

JANE, THE DOWNSTAIRS MAID

Is one of Penelope's seven lovers. Her skin is faintly green and she moves with a strange, swaying gait.

MRS. RICKETS, THE HOUSEKEEPER

Don't forget who *really* owns this house.

SNOOD, THE GARDENER

Never trust anyone with a favorite shovel.

WILSON, THE GAMEKEEPER

Is going to get that parrot if it's the last thing he does.

MRS. DANDERSON, THE COOK

Where the hell are the knives?

CHIVES, THE BUTLER

Did it once.

Manor Events

The aristocracy have three passions: inbreeding, collecting stolen artifacts, and engaging in recreational violence. You must take care as you approach the manor itself and beware of any events in progress, especially a dynastic inheritance struggle.

THE SHOOTING PARTY

There's every chance you could wander onto the property in the middle of a shooting party. This is supposed to be a fun day out in which some servants shake birds out of the bushes while other servants carry and reload guns, all so that the aristocracy can shoot at anything with wings. The shooting party is like the village fête—this is how the nobles weed one another out right in the open. Always assume someone is roaming the grounds with a shotgun looking for long-lost cousin Hugo who just showed up and got top billing in the will. Move fast. Stay low. Don't make a sound until you make it to the door, and preferably not even then.

RENOVATIONS

After the east wing collapsed on some schoolchildren back in the eighties, the villagers made *such* a fuss. Something had to be done. The renovations are still going on and will be going on forever, but there is no money for renovations so they are never going on. The entire manor is held together by scaffolding covered in tapestries and child bones from the east wing incident. Small human skulls are simply perfect for filling holes in the masonry. If only there were a way one could get more . . .

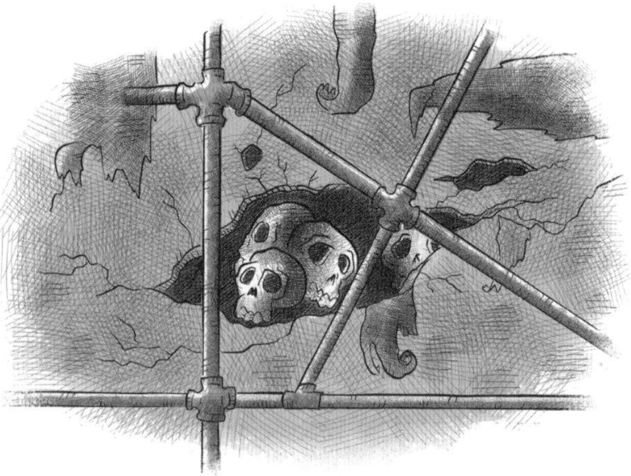

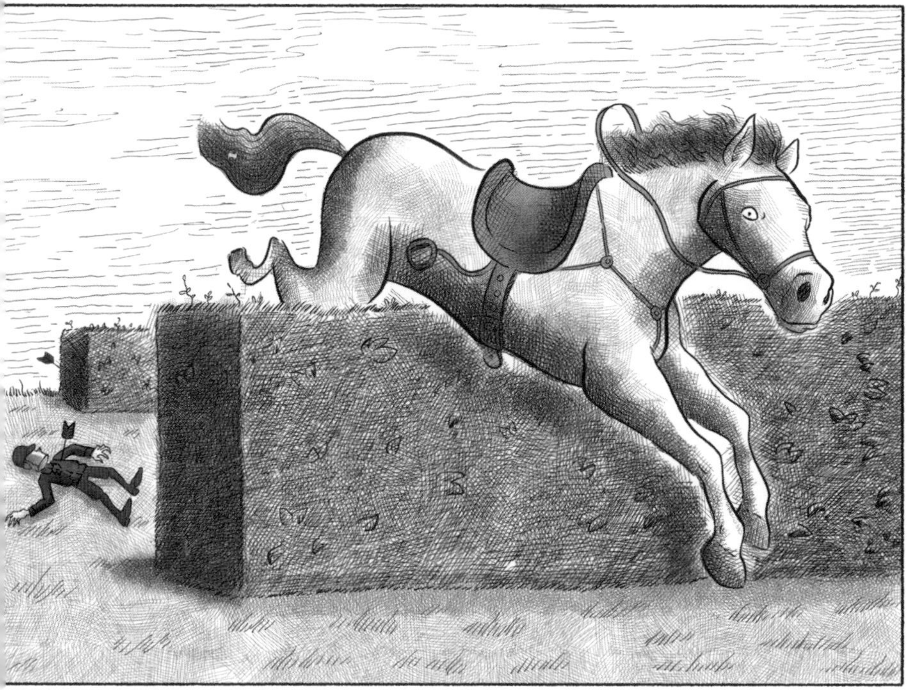

THE WEEKEND HOUSE PARTY

It's so lovely to get out of the city for the weekend and play tennis, have a picnic, do a bit of riding, and commit some adultery. During the day, you will be outside eating and generally recreating. At night, there will be a lot of meaningful stares over the tops of champagne glasses and sneaking from room to room when everyone is supposed to be asleep. What fun! Of course, no one is invited to the manor out of generosity or actual friendship—you are there to be a victim or falsely accused of murder. Enjoy your horsey ride!

THE DINNER PARTY

For when you want to be murdered, but you don't have an entire weekend to spare. This brief festival of poisons and pointy things is a case study in what people can accomplish when they hate everyone around them as much as they hate themselves. Much importance is placed on seating arrangements, because it's crucial to maintain the "deck chairs on the *Titanic*" mood. If you want to eat in a dark, gloomy chamber with many beady eyes trained on you, have dinner in a cave of rabid bats. You'll be safer, and the company will be more enjoyable.

THE OPEN HOUSE

Come in, poors. Look around! You simply *must* see the east wing.

MANOR QUIZ

You have been invited to the manor for the night, and foolishly, you have accepted. Let's see if you'll make it to the morning.

1. You arrive at the gates of the manor at dusk. You hear a dog bark, distant voices, and a cracking sound. Was that . . . a shot? You decide to

a. walk up the main drive toward the house.

b. take a circuitous path through the gardens.

c. turn around and return to the village.

---

a. While it is risky to make yourself an easy target, it's probably best to take the drive. Be quick and zigzag along like you are running from an alligator, just to make it a little harder for them to get a clear shot.

b. You think you are being smart by staying out of sight. You are eaten by the puma in the herb garden. ☠

c. You meet the vicar on the path. ☠

2.

You make it to the front door. Chives takes your bags and directs you to the library, where the family is having a drink before dinner. *What do you do?*

a. Join the family for a drink.

b. Say that you don't need a drink and follow Chives up to the room.

a. A bold choice. Obviously, you won't consume anything. Pour your sherry into a potted plant. Stay away from the walls. If anyone mentions a will, leap out the window.

b. Wisely, you avoid the family's poisoning hour. However, you unwisely opt to follow someone to an unfamiliar location. You fall through a hole in the floor, landing in a pit in the basement, which is filled with the still-soft bodies of other guests. At least you won't decompose alone. ☠

3. Lucy enters the library. Oh, she's disturbed you! Stupid, stupid Lucy! She will go at once . . . unless you don't mind if she stays? Only she wants to borrow a book, you see. It's up on that high shelf. She'll use the ladder, of course, but would you mind awfully steadying it from below? Oh, she's so sorry to trouble you. *How do you respond to Cousin Lucy?*

a. You're very sorry, but you can't.

b. You'd be delighted to.

---

a. You politely decline to hold the ladder, citing obscure religious reasons. Lucy is upset and goes up the ladder alone. She falls and dies. You are found standing over Lucy's body. You are arrested for murder. This is what amounts to a happy ending.

b. You thought you had this one, didn't you? With Lucy up the ladder, she can't knock you off. While you keep an eye on Cousin Lucy, Penelope steals up behind you. Cousin Lucy is another one of Penelope's seven lovers. You have fallen into their trap. You are beaten to death with volume IV of the *Oxford Unabridged Dictionary, Creel-Duzepere,* and your body is taken to the greenhouse for research purposes. ☠

4. Reginald, the child, emerges from an eighteenth-century chest in the hall by the study. He offers you his small clammy hand. He wants to show you his mice.

Do you

a. take his hand and go with him to look at the mice.

b. politely refuse and continue on your way.

c. shove him forcefully back down into the chest and lock it.

---

a. *Don't look at things.* How many times must this be repeated? Do you know how long it takes forty mice to eat a human adult? You're about to find out. ☠

b. Reasonable, but wrong. Reginald does not take rejection well. Do you know how long it takes a human child to eat a human adult? ☠

c. Now you're getting it.

5. You're resting in your room when Aunt Clara slides out from under your bed, whispers something in Latin, and crooks her finger, indicating you should follow her. By the time you get down to the floor, she's gone. In her place is a sliding trap door, partially open. It leads to a crawlspace. *Do you follow her?*

a. Of course not.

b. Immediately.

---

a. You remain in bed, smug, reading your book, congratulating yourself on avoiding the danger. Until the snakes come.

b. It's clear that Aunt Clara Knows Something, and the first and primary rule is that you never associate with people who Know Things. Also, following someone into a crawlspace is a bad idea, generally. But Aunt Clara has survived in this house for a long time; she knows what's what. You slide down into the musty crawlspace and follow her crab-like form as she makes her way between the floors. You drop down into an empty wall cavity behind the family portrait gallery. From there, you peer out through the eyeholes and watch as Marianne kills Roger with a dagger and shoves his body up the chimney. Aunt Clara looks at you reassuringly and smiles. You have an ally. She will help you escape. She is . . . covered in snakes. They have fallen through the walls. Oh god, no, not the snakes, not the snakes. Oh well.

Final Thoughts

A few final points before concluding this volume.

WILLS

Given what you have learned, you may be tempted to make out your will before you go on your trip. Do not do this. The residents can sniff out a fresh will like a pig sniffs out truffles. It does not matter that the residents are likely not mentioned in your will; the scent brings out a murderous impulse. The moment you step into the village, they will have you on a pike, and they won't know why. Let your relatives fight over your collection of meerschaum pipes, if it comes to that.

ACCOMMODATIONS

It is usual to make lodging arrangements in advance. You must not do this. No one can know you are coming–that gives them time to plan. Ideally, you should not stay anywhere. If you can, remain awake and moving during the entirety of your stay. If you must rest, try to find a hollow log or disused shed. Sleep during the day, in short bursts. If you insist on staying at the local inn, pay with a credit card and make it known in an abnormally loud voice that *lots of people know where you are and are expecting you to come back*. Push furniture against the door. Close the curtains. Pry some floorboards up beneath the bed and burrow. Worry.

DINING

One must eat while traveling, which is a pity. Try to hold off on consuming anything while you are in the village or at the manor. Fill up on nonfood items, such as paper, leaves, or grass. Drink from puddles or catch rain in your hat. Certainly you must *pretend* to eat and drink because the locals will soon sense something is wrong if you eat all the newspapers and lap up puddles on the streets. They will kill you just for being weird.

GUIDEBOOKS

Whatever you do, do not allow a guidebook to lull you into a false sense of security, especially one that advertises itself as a way of avoiding the deadly pitfalls of an English Murder Village. While you've got your nose buried in a book, someone could be sneaking up behind you, perhaps someone who wrote a book enumerating the various ways you could be murdered in an English Murder Village. Someone who gave you fair warning at the beginning and told you to heed its advice and dispose of this book. Someone who filled the book with amusing pictures that would make it all seem like a delightful wheeze, ensuring you would pay no mind to the sound of the door creaking open and the footsteps behind you . . .

Go ahead. Turn around. Say, "Oh, it's you."

FIN